T0244913

ALSO BY AUGUST KLEINZAHLER

POETRY

Snow Approaching on the Hudson

Before Dawn on Bluff Road / Hollyhocks in the Fog

The Hotel Oneira

Sleeping It Off in Rapid City: Poems, New and Selected

The Strange Hours Travelers Keep

Live from the Hong Kong Nile Club: Poems 1975–1990

Green Sees Things in Waves

Red Sauce, Whiskey and Snow

Like Cities, Like Storms

Earthquake Weather

On Johnny's Time

Storm over Hackensack

A Calendar of Airs

The Sausage Master of Minsk

PROSE

Sallies, Romps, Portraits, and Send-Offs: Selected Prose, 2000–2016

Music: I–LXXIV

Cutty, One Rock: Low Characters and Strange Places, Gently Explained

A
HISTORY OF
WESTERN
MUSIC

A
HISTORY OF
WESTERN
MUSIC

POEMS

AUGUST
KLEINZAHLER

FARRAR, STRAUS AND GIROUX

NEW YORK

Farrar, Straus and Giroux
120 Broadway, New York 10271

Printed in the United States of America
First edition, 2024

Library of Congress Cataloging-in-Publication Data
Names: Kleinzahler, August, author.
Title: A history of Western music : poems / August Kleinzahler.
Description: First edition. | New York : Farrar, Straus and Giroux, 2024.
Identifiers: LCCN 2024008321 | ISBN 9780374611927 (paperback)
Subjects: LCSH: Music—Western countries—Poetry. | LCGFT: Poetry.
Classification: LCC PS3561.L38285 H57 2024 | DDC 811/.54—dc23/eng/
    20240226
LC record available at https://lccn.loc.gov/2024008321

Designed by Gretchen Achilles

Our books may be purchased in bulk for promotional, educational,
or business use. Please contact your local bookseller or the Macmillan Corporate
and Premium Sales Department at 1-800-221-7945, extension 5442, or by email at
MacmillanSpecialMarkets@macmillan.com.

www.fsgbooks.com
Follow us on social media at @fsgbooks

1 3 5 7 9 10 8 6 4 2

For Marcy

Man, if you have to ask what it is,
you'll never know.

—LOUIS ARMSTRONG

CONTENTS

CHAPTER 63 (WHITNEY HOUSTON) 3

CHAPTER 88 (ZIPOLI AND THE PARAGUAY REDUCTIONS) 6

CHAPTER 29 (IN MEMORIAM THOM GUNN) 8

CHAPTER 60 (LITTLE C.R. AND JUDY) 9

CHAPTER 74 (EURYTHMICS) 11

CHAPTER 13 (MONK) 14

CHAPTER 49 (McPHEE'S GAMELAN) 17

CHAPTER 72 (BARTLEBY) 21

CHAPTER 11 (SPOLETO) 23

CHAPTER 77 (30, RUE DULUTH) 27

CHAPTER 18 (BILL EVANS) 30

CHAPTER 1 (MAHLER/SINATRA) 32

CHAPTER 73 (DANCE, DANCE, DANCE) 35

CHAPTER 9 (BLUE AT 4 P.M.) 37

CHAPTER 44 (BEBOP) 38

CHAPTER 5 (HYPER-BERCEUSE: 3 A.M.) 41

CHAPTER 12 (INGRAM MARSHALL, *FOG TROPES*) 43

CHAPTER 42 (CASPIAN LAKE, VERMONT) 47

CHAPTER 3 (THE MAGIC FLUTE) 49

CHAPTER 4 (THE MONKEY OF LIGHT) 52

CHAPTER 33 ("COMING ON THE HUDSON": WEEHAWKEN) 55

CHAPTER 40 (EXILE) 57

CHAPTER 38 (ROSE EXILE) 60

CHAPTER 21 (APRIL IN PARIS) 62

CHAPTER 81 (SARANAC LAKE) 65

CHAPTER 6 (ODEON) 67

CHAPTER 57 (ROUTE 4) 69

CHAPTER 31 (BAY LULLABY) 71

CHAPTER 99 (FINIS) 73

Acknowledgments 79

A
HISTORY OF
WESTERN
MUSIC

CHAPTER 63

(WHITNEY HOUSTON)

They follow you around the store, these power ballads,
you and the women with their shopping carts filled with eggs,
cookies, 90 fl. oz. containers of antibacterial dishwashing liquid,
buffeting you sideways like a punishing wind.

You stand, almost hypnotized, at the rosticceria counter
staring at the braised lamb shanks, the patterns
those tiny, coagulated rivulets of fat make,
both knees about to go out from under you.

—*Can I help you, sir?*
No, no, thank you, I'm afraid not . . .

It's mostly the one woman who writes these things,
a petite, almost perpetually somber, brunette
in her L.A. studio, undecorated, two cats,
traffic coursing up and down the boulevard outside,

curtains drawn against the unrelenting sun.
Because of your *unconventional* lifestyle
you have been shopping among women your entire life,
young mothers and matrons,

almost no other males around except staff and seniors,
the old men squinching their eyes, scowling at the prices.

What sort of life have you led
that you find yourself, an adult male of late middle age,

about to weep among the avocados and citrus fruits
in a vast, overlit room next to a bosomy Cuban grandma
with her sparkly, extravagant eyewear?
It's good that your parents are no longer alive.

It's a simple formula, really: verse, verse, chorus
(and don't take too long to get there),
verse, chorus, bridge, solo, if any,
chorus (good chance of key modulation here, really gets 'em)—

electric keyboard, soaring guitar, likely a string part or two.
There's no telling how much that woman is worth,
a "misunderstood Jewish girl" from Van Nuys.
How would one go about making love to someone like that,

sitting alone in her studio all day, shades drawn, two cats,
writing these songs of tortured love,
up to the tips of her waders in self-immolation,
often keeping at it well into the night?

Celine Dion, Cher, Michael Bolton, Faith Hill, Toni Braxton—
knocking you back one after another, all morning and afternoon,
at least until the men arrive after work. I don't know why.
Perhaps it has to do with the "emotional nature" of women.

You, you're breathing all funny, nearly paralyzed.
But there's one song they almost never play

and I'll tell you why: it's the one Dolly Parton wrote,
not the brunette, but it's not Dolly who's doing the singing,

it's the one who just died. Because if they played that one,
it wouldn't be just you dying in aisle 5.
All the girls would be dropping there like it was sarin gas
pouring from the speakers up there hidden behind the lights.

(ZIPOLI AND THE PARAGUAY REDUCTIONS)

The rivercraft moves slowly upriver in the heart of Terra Magellanica,
this forestland of earthquakes, hurricanes and volcanic eruptions,
sitting low in the mud-colored water, laden with its cargo
of appoggiaturas, mordents, sarabandes, gavottes and trills,
along with Domenico Zipoli in his black cassock, late of Rome, Florence, Bologna
and Naples, scene of his famous contretemps with Scarlatti père.

A white miasmic vapor covers the river and forest until burning off midday.
Large clumps of water hyacinths and water lilies floating by
seething with venomous snakes like Medusa hair,
endless swampland, seas of pampas grass, forests of jacaranda.
With dusk settling in, the burrowing, metallic roar of cicadas,
and later in the depths of night, the sounds of a jaguar rending the flesh

of a sleeping Guarani or wayward Christian enjoying a tinkle behind a tree.
Susan Alexander-Max is recording Zipoli's 1716 *Sonate d'Intavolatura*
on an original Cristofori *gravicembalo col piano e forte*
in one of the André Mertens Galleries at the Metropolitan Museum of Art
on a beautiful fall afternoon in 1992, the famous entrance steps of the museum
littered with tourists and locals taking in the sun and grand old mansions

across the way, Beaux Arts, Second Empire, foliage in high color in Central Park.
The most beautiful keyboard timbre on earth, along with Silbermann's fortepiano,
1749, dismissed out of hand by Johannes Sebastian Bach as "insufficient,"
falling somewhere between the harpsichord and modern piano, most deliciously.

Domenico Zipoli never heard or played on either, more's the pity, but not for us,
one disc, and one only, currently available from Amazon for $99, a steal.

These suites, in B minor, C major and D minor, published in 1716,
with their "exquisitely timed modulations, tuneful, concise and never dry."
Alligators bask, half-submerged, in the shallows along the riverbanks.
Our Soldier of Christ penetrates ever deeper into the green enamel sheen
of the tropical rainforest, this "inland China" between the two great rivers,
lianas with their yellow, red and purple clusters of blossoms, hanging

like enormous bunches of grapes overhead within reach of the boat,
monkeys and parrots chattering away, thickets of wild orange, lemon and lime,
red earth the violent tropical rains turn into a red paste.
Scarlet and blue macaws soar overhead like brightly colored hawks,
crimson carpets of verbena, devil's trumpet, yellow datura.
The dark young Guarani boy in white, swinging the censer, tower bells sounding,

and the organ blast of a diapason reverberating throughout the jungle,
then slowly subsiding, until swallowed by insect whirr and birdsong.

CHAPTER 29

(IN MEMORIAM THOM GUNN)

(after Johnny Mercer)

I took a trip on a plane
And I thought about you
I lunched alone in the rain
And I thought about you

One streetcar, then two, disappearing from view
A tortured dream
The fog blowing in, canceling all that had been
Going street by street
Like a cop on his beat

Over the Great Salt Lake
Yeah, I thought about you
But when I pulled down the shade
Man, I really got blue

I snuck a peek at the clouds
Muttered something aloud
Something I once said to you

We do as we have to
I thought about you

(LITTLE C.R. AND JUDY)

A good lad, Christopher, a tad pensive, or watchful, for one so young.
A bookworm too, if ever there was one: perhaps a career in law
or some sort of scholarly pursuit or other, but surely a hopeless fit
for the give-and-take of Fleet Street or the City or as an estate agent.
Still, a well-behaved and temperate child, pleasant enough company,
but just this very moment struggling, and failing, to squelch a giggle
ten thousand feet above the Persian Gulf in one of only eleven seats
on a de Havilland 104 Dove, which will presently be passing
over the rocky terrain, salt pans and limestone formations of Qatar,
beginning its descent only fifteen minutes after having taken off,
the hydraulic whine of the landing gear making ready to extend.
I would never have characterized the Reids as a prim couple, not at all,
but clearly discomfited by the singing coming from first class
behind the black curtain from what sounded to be a very drunk
American woman warbling in a stricken vibrato, a familiar tune,
difficult to make out from the slurring and occasional hiccup.
(Shall I go ahead and tell you the title? I don't suppose it matters . . .)
But a favorite of hers, a kind of party trick after she's had a few,
or more than a few. And how much is a few? Or a few too many?
You too might be inclined to burst into song now and then
if you had pipes like hers and that was what you loved to do best, sing,
better than the rest, a voice the world has delighted to for twenty years.
The problem was the rest: poor thing, poor, poor thing—
the horrible stage mom, Sam Goldwyn, Artie Shaw, I'll spare the litany.
Judy Davis, the divine Judy Davis, gave a splendid performance of her

as she began to come apart in 1960 (which is right about now, isn't it?),
swollen, nearly broke, the marriage to Sid on the rocks.
And then the 2019 bio-drama with Renée Zellweger: oh MY GOD.
—*What's with the tears, sweetie?* We are thirty thousand feet above America,
returning home from Ponta Delgada, its verdure and tea plantations,
waves crashing over the breakwater in front of the hotel . . .
The de Havilland has landed safely and the Reids prepare to disembark.
—*Who was that woman up front?* Mr. Reid inquires of the captain.
She appears to be keeping her seat for yet another leg of her journey.
To Oman? To belt out a medley of greatest hits for Said Bin Taimur,
thirteenth Sultan of Muscat and Oman, a monster and fool like the rest,
but rumored to have become a great fan of American pop culture
on a visit to the country in 1938 where he enjoyed a guided tour
of the Metro-Goldwyn-Mayer lot and the filming of *The Wizard of Oz*.
He had never been so moved, that lovely child singing the theme song,
a beautiful contralto, even then. It has stayed with him all these years:

    Somewhere over the . . .

CHAPTER 74

(E U R Y T H M I C S)

Odd, unsettling somehow, visiting here again after so many years,
traveling through town at this hour,
the Baixa nearly deserted, then along the river, the lights of the bridge
    blurred by rain,
just me and the consul's driver:
customized Citroën C4 Aircross Picasso, outsize smoked-glass windows,
upholstered like the inside of a leather queen's crypt, brown Bavarian bull hide.
Might as well be in a glass bathyscaphe or slow-motion pneumatic tube
forcing its passage through a tunnel of oil.

I mean, how different is this from the last time,
way back when, before our *anthem* hit the charts? It's still in everyone's earbuds,
even here: the *fidalgos* in $500 jeans, the monsignors in their black cassocks,
    purple trim, the senhora ladling out the *caldo verde* and *feijoada*.
In those days she would have been dressed in black.
You lived on that kale and potato soup, and with that bottle of *piri-piri*
you carried around everywhere we went. And me, custard cups.
They cost pennies in those days, with the *fascistas* still in power,
at least for a few more months. They were watching us, that crew. Not sure why.
We'd run into Saramago at the *pastelaria* all the time, remember?
He lived nearby. He wasn't famous yet, just finishing up the *Blimunda* novel,
the one with Scarlatti. He'd buy us both a *galão* now and then, sweet man.
I can't imagine he had much more than we did.

Nor we; famous, that is. Not quite yet. It wasn't until the band let me sing.

No one was much into drum machines then,

at least not how we went about it, and that big bass synthesizer sound,

the two of us tap-tapping on part-filled milk bottles in time to the chorus.

I forget who it was dreamt that one up,

clink-clink, clink-clink, each bottle a different level of water, different pitch.

But it worked. Blow me, it worked . . .

What were we, twenty-two, twenty-three?

We walked all the way down from the summer palace.

Dark green avenues, fern colonnades, those ponds with water lilies . . .

Lord Georgie-Porgie wasn't half-wrong. It was like Eden, but even Eden can
     get old.

We were starving when we found that hole-in-the-wall just off the square,

and the bossy little owner with his charcoal brazier.

He nearly dragged us in there and made us sit still for what seemed like an hour,

grilling those chunks of cuttlefish, basting and basting them in their own ink.

You squealed like a little pig later on when you got a good look at your tongue.

—I'm gonna die, I'm gonna die!

It rained most every day that January, just like it's raining now,

the Terreiro do Paço nearly underwater.

I'd never been anywhere like this before. I don't know that I'd really been
     anywhere.

Climbing up all those slippery cobbled steps every night to that pensão the
     nuns ran,

half-pissed, the white peacocks shrieking in the castle garden

and the sound they made in the rain. It moves me still, this place,

the jumble of pastel doorways with their sagging jambs and worn stone sills.

The people too, so modest and obliging, a bit melancholy—

no, not so much melancholy, subdued, perhaps, a lid on top.
They do fancy their hats, all right, the old gents.

We clung together like children then.
And you could be so awful, especially if your dick wasn't in me or you weren't
    drinking.
I'd cry and cry, not because of how you were or what you said.
I felt like I was always melting inside.

Yeah, yeah, sure—*But oft, in lonely rooms, and 'mid the din / of towns and
    cities . . .*
My apologies, Mr. Chalmers, you did your best . . .

You know how water finds its way through a seam in the roof.
I mean, do I really want to split open again like a sodden aubergine?
Does anyone need to see that again?

These drives to the airport are all the same, no matter what town you're in.
—Luis, darling, can you turn up the sound a bit? You know who that is, don't you?
Of course, luv, of course you do.

CHAPTER 13

(M O N K)

The large Black man is dancing
He is dancing in his head
On the stage of the Salle Pleyel
And the Parisians are watching
As he takes one step to the left
But look, his foot is not touching
The ground, as if it's too hot
Or cold, or not to be found there at all
Then slamming it down
And spinning round
Like a drunk in his funny hat

The large Black man is dancing
On the stage of the Salle Pleyel
He has gotten up from the piano
And begun his silly dance
Lurching first one way, then . . .
Wait, he is changing his mind
Frozen there in space, on just one leg
His drummer and bass, Pierre
That is, and Claude, puzzling through
What he has left behind
Soldiering on, regardless
Wondering where they misplaced the time
On the stage of the Salle Pleyel

The large Black man is dancing
Dancing in his head
On the stage of the Salle Pleyel
And hundreds of French are watching him
Twitch or swat
Away an imaginary chord in order to make room
For the next, with a pirouette
Courtly as a maître d' on roller skates

The large Black man, the large
Black man is dancing
And the Parisians are watching
Nervously. But the drummer, Pierre
That is, and Claude on bass
Are beginning to get it
They are watching the Black man's dance
And think they've found it
Relax, *mes chers*
We are nearing the end of the tune

The Black, Black man is dancing
Dancing in his head
On the stage of the grand *théâtre*
And the lovers of jazz are there
They are out there in force
Watching the Black man from America
Watching the Black man dance
It is 1954
And the tune is "Trinkle, Tinkle"
What are they to do

What to make
Of the Black man up there dancing
Is he *fou*
Does he not know where he is or who
Is in the audience watching
There is the editor of *Jazz Hot*
Section C, aisle 12, seat 2
He will be confused, no
Is he being made the fool
What are they all to do

Pierre and Claude, the drummer
That is, and the contrabass
They think: OK, I've got it
Where the accents drop
Where not
And those very weird spaces between
(*Ha, ha, ha*, but not really)

The large Black man
In his coat and his tie
And the funny little hat
And crazy grin
The large Black man is
DANCING

CHAPTER 49

(M C P H E E ' S   G A M E L A N)

The overtones drift out over the lake
from the direction of the east-facing pavilion,

gathering themselves into a tree of tiny mirrors,
mirrors and gold foil,

suspended above the water's surface—

late sun through heavy foliage,

the clangorous exhalations
dissolving into the low sounds of wind
on water, on nearby *lalang* grass.

Frangipani and incense—
the gods have been summoned:

"Sea of Honey," "Some False Silver,"
"Monkey Looks at Himself in the Water" . . .

After a slow and chant-like bass
the melody ranges freely, coming and going,

in and out of shimmering arabesques
that ring in the treble as though beaten out
on a thousand wee anvils, xylophones clicking like hail.

—*How shall the gongs be tuned?* asked the smith:
Deep-voiced, in the tuning called "Brave Sea,"
or shriller, in the pitch called "Burnt Tamarind"?

—*What is best for the Gamelan of Samara, the Love God?*
asked the other.

—*"A Field of Flowering Pandanus,"*
said the smith, after a moment's thought.
—*That is the softest and most profound.*

Sentences, too, must float,
if you follow what I mean.

Chopin floats; Schubert, as well.
What is it exactly?
I can't quite put my finger on it.

His eyes met mine in a glance of insolent penetration.
—*The air is salubrious here*, he remarked,
looking out across the valley.

Then there was another tuning,
beautiful and rare.
I had sometimes heard it down by the sea, near Sanur.

The changes among tones very slight,
imparting to the music a sweetly melancholic air.
I believe it is called "the scale of midnight."

Her dishes were endless:
skewers of birds no bigger than bumblebees,
and strangest of all,
small green packages in the shape of cigarettes,
inside them toasted coconut and larvae of dragonflies.

The faint chime of a g'nder
with its floating, disembodied sound,
from a nearby veranda:

a single musician playing softly to himself,
waiting for the others to return.

Nutmeg, gardenias, burnt feathers . . .

—*What style!* the old man said,
listening as a tremulous voice rose up, into the air,
above the faint sound of drums.

It was the famous singer from Buleleng—Miss Lemonade.

Kenong, Reyong, Kendang, Trompang, Calung, Gong

Languor and reverie in these chiming tones,
some soft and liquid, some like the notes of a flute,

others full, like the tones of an organ:
perfume, legend, secrecy.

We stood there staring at the water
while a boy tossed scarlet hibiscus into a pool.

Sentences, too, must float . . .

(B A R T L E B Y)

A rounded and orbicular sound to it, and rings
like unto bullion—
                    the description so plagued
Mme Cornichon's memory as she adjusted her slip
before settling herself onto the furze

for what she hoped would be reverie.
Ants scattered, two large beetles as well,
of such a kind as she had never seen,
enormous, their plates giving off an iridescent sheen

as they scuttled willy-nilly in slow-motion alarm.
Above her, hidden among leaves, the chatter
of wrens and grackles was as a fretful orison
to her in her repose, but the music that ranged

most freely through her being was Ravel's "Miroirs,"
especially so "Oiseaux tristes," suggested by the song
of a blackbird *but in the mood* of a "bird lost

in the overwhelming blackness of a forest

during the hottest hour of summer." Ah,
she remembered being awash with glissandi and arpeggios

in the salon of the Princesse Edmond de Polignac,
one afternoon with the skies outside ready to burst—

and they did. But drenched as she was, shoes ruined,
she barely noticed, still so transported
by the tapestry of sound—hypnotized. Regrettably,
she took sick, and yet it was the princess,

not she, who succumbed to a bronchial complaint.
What would ever become of the great stuffed owl
suspended above the divan, the Art Nouveau sideboard
and chinoiserie? Blessedly, the illness was swift.

And the *Pavane* . . . What was it Ravel himself said
after a too too *adagio* performance years later?
Something about that it was the princess, not
the *Pavane*, that was supposed to be dead.

CHAPTER 11

(SPOLETO)

The beauty—
the way the swallows gather around the Duomo
for a few moments at dusk then scatter,
darting across the Vale
with its checkerboard pastels dissolving into smoke
along with the hills beyond.
We saw it that one time from the maestro's apartments,
through a little oval window above the piazza
while that awful American baritone—what's his name—
was mauling the love duet with Poppea at the end,
and she so wickedly angelic, a Veronese angel . . .
When de Kooning, drunk, crashed into us,
then the lot of us staggering off to that bar
overlooking the Ponte delle Torri,
winding up drinking in the dawn outside Vincenzo's.
I remember the violist and cor anglais
enjoying some passion in the doorway.
Didn't they later marry? Perhaps not.
The mezzo from Winston-Salem—
I won't tell you her name; you'll know it.
She was only a girl then, pretending
to be native, with her Neapolitan accent
and dark looks, that extravagant manner
and big laugh the divas all seem to cultivate,
peeking to check if her act was really coming off.

These actresses and stage performers are always a trial.

By the time you finally get them home

and properly unwound, the cockerels and tweety birds

already hard at it, they either collapse

into tears or fall dead away, shoes still on,

snoring and farting like drunken sailors.

But that night, that night it was the English poet

(now much beloved but in those days known as the *Badger*)

was after her, her and her friend,

the pianist from Ravenna, the quieter of the two,

the heart-attack brunette, renowned for her Saint-Saëns.

You'll know her name too, and the recordings

she made later on with the mezzo of the Schubert lieder.

But then they were just kids, figuring it out,

suffering dainty little sips

of that tall dreadful yellow drink, a favorite here,

meanwhile taking the measure of it all,

as if rehearsing for a more serious moment down the road.

The cunning, energy and fortitude of these creatures

almost never fail to horrify and amaze,

especially two thoroughbreds like these.

One might easily revile them for it,

but as well revile some magnificent cat in the grass

scanning the savanna for meat.

Anyhow, the *Badger* was on form that night.

You wouldn't know him. He was young then,

really quite presentable, even appealing, I suppose,

with a shock of blond hair

and that pale, distracted, feral look he chose to wear.

I don't know that I've ever known a human being to drink like that.

I mean now the swollen old cunt could pass for Uncle Bertie
but in those days . . . So now the *Badger*
was well along into his routine: a few bons mots,
feigned interest, the scholarly quote and the rest,
then his signature:

     —I don't suppose a fuck would be out of the question?
The girls took no notice, giggling between themselves
and the inevitable band of toffs and toff-y rent boys
who gather round these affairs. Love culture,
the toffs, can't live without it: mother's milk,
penicillin for the syphilitic.
And where would we be without them: their dinners,
soirees, art openings,
wives we could so generously appall?
Simply can't get enough of it, the toffs. Or the wives.
So this particular evening the *Badger* was dead on chart,
watching, waiting, picking his spot:

     —Ha-ha, listen, I don't suppose . . .
when just then Signor Cor Anglais struggles to his feet,
a humongous hard-on like a prow in advance of the rest,
and proceeds to blow a heavenly riff from Bruckner,
one of those alphorn bits the Bavarians so adore.
Well now, this provoked an enormous display
on the part of the toffs, sissies, remittance men,
expats—those orphans, those sorry, deracinated ghosts—
the lot of them in the ruins of black tie,
shrieking like nine-year-olds at the circus
when the clown takes a flop, out of their gourds,
full up with helium, Eeeeeeeeeeeeeeeeeee—
la vie bohème, right out there on the Corso,

a moment to be savored and regurgitated for years to come,
when the Cor Anglais decides to pass out,
Signora Viola all over him, beside herself,
like the final scene from—well, you name it—
the toffs, etc., carrying on like they had a ringside seat
at Krakatoa erupting on New Year's Eve;
and then I hear the mezzo—all of us,
everything else falling away, the air rippling with it—
up on her feet, singing the "Adagiati Poppea,"
in Monteverdi's *L'Incoronazione*, warning
of the iniquitous union ahead, but sung
with such tenderness, an unearthly sweetness.
The entire street falling silent around us,
and the *Badger* just standing there like the rest,
hypnotized, but now his face gone slack—
astonishment? epiphany? grief?—but clearly shaken
and—unimaginably out of character—about to weep.

(3 0 , R U E   D U L U T H)

—*Elvis is dead*, the radio said,
where it sat behind a fresh-baked loaf of bread
and broken link of *kolbász*
fetched only lately from Boucherie Hongroise:
Still Life Without Blue Pitcher.
I read that piece of meat as if I were Chaim Soutine,
with its capillaries and tiny kernels of fat
bound up in its burnt-sienna casing.
There and then the motif came to me
that would anchor my early masterwork, Opus 113.
No? I'll hum the first few bars.

The window was small,
and set low on the wall. Little out there to see,
only the legs of pedestrians below the knee.
Captive, a prisoner nearly, inside the ochre room,
as the radio poured forth this terrible news:
—*KING ELVIS IS DEAD*
his flesh empurpled, the giant gold medallion,
his lolling tongue bitten nearly in two.

I took note, the time was propitious for soup
even amidst the bulletins and updates, and then made ready
with the preliminary slow-mo casting about that attends
the act of creation,

a length of sausage readily at hand.
Soup-making always seemed to settle me back then.

Those with whom I lived considered me vain,
excepting the Lady M,
with whom I tirelessly played,
Parcheesi, Scrabble, less circumscribed games.
She would have bought for me a giant gold medallion
could she have managed the expense,
if only I would let her.

Presently the soup was the color of the room;
everything around me, the walls, the air,
varying shades of ochre,
but pebbled with paprika-colored nuggets.

They say he existed on Tuinal and cheddar,
his blood turned to sludge,
odds & ends from this snack or that buried deep inside him,
dating all the way back to *Blue Hawaii,*
the fat around his neck like a collar of *boudin blanc.*

Every so often he'd soil his white cape,
and only, it turns out, in Vegas and while onstage.
Now, that's what I call a showman.

Both afternoon and summer were drawing to a close
while the soup thickened on the stove,
the unlit room darkening by degree.

The radio resumed its regular programming,
and, as always seemed the case that hour of the day,
the *Gymnopédies* by Satie.

(BILL EVANS)

He stared for hours
at the cat
taking his ease under the calla leaf
or fog
pour in late afternoon
whelming the tower on the hill

how   bird   truck   or shout
wind & light
scored day the way the music roll
in a nickelodeon's scored
and what it plays in the mind

along with that afternoon's
first set, June '61
the faint tinkle of glasses, muffled
conversations, a cough

and he launches into it, LaFaro's
bass coming in
right behind him, then Motian's
simmering brushes

the room unready
something out of the ordinary

about to befall them
just another leisurely Sunday
afternoon, taking refuge
from the heat
rising off the sidewalk

    "My Foolish Heart"

playing on his stereo now, here
in the Haight, thirty years later, again
and again
through the dying afternoon
the cat, the palm tree swathed in trumpet
vine, tufts
of cloud floating past the radio tower
on the hill

unable to move, overcome
if you will
fennel lobelia
             shadow & cloud
however many times it takes

CHAPTER I

(MAHLER/SINATRA)

April of that year in the one country
was unusually clear
and with *brisk* northeasterlies
"straight from the Urals."
Their ancient regent at long last succumbed
and was laid to rest after much ceremony.
Sinatra was everywhere that spring,
in the hotel lobbies, toilets, shops—
"Fly Me to the Moon," "You Make Me Feel
So Young," name it.
On TV a computer-generated Weimaraner
sang "I did it my way"
in a gravelly baritone.

                        —He only weighed 130 pounds,
Ava Gardner was said to have remarked,
soaking wet.
But a hundred of those pounds was cock.

Whereas the season before
in the other country to the west
no matter into which room you walked
it would have been the *heart-wrenching adagietto*
from Mahler's Symphony No. 5.
Only a small country,
it had endured a long, *famously tragic* history.

Still, it was more than passing strange,
not halfway through your plate of mussels,
the tremblingly _____ *adagietto*
was showering you with the debris
of Gustav Mahler's *tortured* soul. True,
wife Alma was a troublesome slut;
we know this of her and choose to forgive.
But what of this late Romantic excess,
this anthem of the Hapsburg twilight,
in a cruelly served and windswept land?

We had only lately come over the Sally Gap
across the bogland, down through the glen,
and were walking slowly
along the Lower Lake of Glendalough.
Afternoon had turned toward evening,
and with it came a chill.
And with the chill a mist
had begun to gather over the lake.
—*This is a haunted place*, I heard her say.

It was quiet then. We were the last ones there.
Only a patch of birdsong. Only the wind.
Unheeded, from somewhere *out of the blue*,
—*Liberace*, she said, and nothing more.
We continued on our walk and listened,
if just to the silence.
This would have been the hour Saint Kevin knew
and savored
before retreating to the Gatehouse

and into the monastery for evening prayer.
One can imagine a stillness forming around him there
like those halos of gold or ochre
that surround the sacred figures in *ancient* frescoes.

Much as they do with "Lee"
in one of his brocaded lamé jumpsuits
with its sequins catching the spotlights,
enorbing the performer in brilliant rays
as he smiles *coquettishly* to the Vegas crowd
then turns to deliver the first
in a series of *thunderous* glissandi,
somehow finding his way back
to a climactic, *magnificently rousing* chorus
of that million seller
and *timeless classic*

> "Moon River."

CHAPTER 73

(DANCE, DANCE, DANCE)

The four of us would make that little house shake, dancing the night away,
perched there at the foot of the block, right above the cove,
wind blowing at thirty knots, rain peppering the windows like BB pellets.
It's a wonder we didn't tip, the house and us with it, onto the rocky strand below.
Stax/Volt, King Records' R & B stalwarts: "Finger Poppin' Time," "Chain of
    Fools,"
you taking a solo turn on "Poppa's Got a Brand New Bag," twitching
to beat the band in your *Isadora-gone-spastic-with-rabies* mode,
drunkenly crashing into walls, knocking the furniture every which way.
I still can't figure out how your wee John slept through it all, if he really did.
He somehow made it to Yale, I heard, then studied law. No fault of yours . . .
His mother found a proper gent once she managed to unload you, that's how.
You dear, impossible, most thoughtless of men. —*What did the doctor tell you?*
—*He told me I was in perfect health—for a 60-year-old.* You were then 25.
But somehow lasted another 50, which would have made you 525 in dog years,
an image to reckon with, those tight black curls gone white, the same mad glare.
If only you'd been with it near the end, able to see on television the apotheosis
of your contempt for nearly everything take over center stage and set up shop.
You taught me most everything I know about music, at least the raw stuff:
the Dixie Hummingbirds, the Louvin Brothers, Ralph Stanley singing
"I'm a Man of Constant Sorrow" you claimed made the paint peel off your walls.
We'd always finish off the evening with Séamus Ennis, of County Ennis,
skirling his way through "Kiss the Maid Behind the Barrel" on his uilleann
    pipes,
the only sound that could bore its way through that amber veil of Bushmills.

You'd have made the best DJ ever to be found in this sad old world, ever, ever,

if only you weren't such a hopeless shambles, and a station might be found

to accommodate your lurchings: Furtwängler on the heels of Guitar Shorty.

I remember one night we all danced so hard the house seemed to shift,

if only a bit. It wasn't much of a house, I suppose. Still, the landlord wasn't happy.

We danced and danced the nights away on that green, wet, sleepy, nowhere isle.

I recall no better or harder dancing, you wobbling, but in command, at the helm.

CHAPTER 9

(BLUE AT 4 P.M.)

The burnish of late afternoons
as winter ends—
this sadness coming on in waves is not round
and sweet
as the doleful cello

but jagged, intent
finding out places to get through the way the wind
tries seams
and cracks in the old house, making
the furnace kick on

or the way his trumpet
sharks
through cloud and paradise shoal, nosing
out the dark fillet
to tear apart and drink his own

CHAPTER 44

(BEBOP)

YAHTZEE   *YAHTZEE*   *YAHTZEE*

At Rapunzel's Fungible Ball
The most glittery jittery gala of all

The Vedettes & Babettes
Scarfed down crêpes suzettes
Orange butter spray-painting the walls

What a feast, what a fete
Scamps vamping away till last call

YAHTZEE   *YAHTZEE*

HIPPITY-HOPSIE

Strambunzella's combustible tattersall
A headache to even recall
So much effervescing Buzette lost first her *courgette*
Her silver barrette
Her earrings next you might say
Her bearings wobbling as if ready to . . .

At Rapunzel's jungly . . .
Even the discreet left their feet
Rapunzel's Fungible . . .

Varlets at the gate loath to wait
Tantrums broke plates—
A proper stromboli-strewn brawl

YAHTZEE   *YAHTZEE*

SWEET-DEW-DROPSIE

Quiddity's itch nay timidity's twitch toggle-switch bobble
Rob Pete to pay Gobble *tout de suite* move your feet try not to fall

YAHTZEE   *YAHTZEE*

REET PETITE-TATER-TOTSIE

A ramp'd up dance call it *cha-cha-faux-bocci*

CHOC-A-LATTA-CHOC-A-LITA-CHOC-A-TIKKA-LOTTA

BOMBA-GA-BONGA-GA-BUM-GUM-GA-HUBBLE-BUBBLE-SAMBA

STROMBOLITO ESCONDITO

AB-SOL-EET-LY TUTTI-FRUTTI

HAMMUROOBI

PEEK-A-BOOCHIE

SLOW-FAUX-BOCCI

Syncopated commotion   addled emu shunned

YAHTZEE   *YAHTZEE*   *YAHTZEE*

Rapunzel Rapunzel let down your . . .

The hottest ticket of all

Glittery Jittery

Rapunzel's Fungible Ball

CHAPTER 5

(HYPER-BERCEUSE: 3 A.M.)

Imagine in all the debris of space
The countless trade names
    Jugurtha   *Tuolumne*   *Chert-Farms*
Some of these belong to you
Can you tell which ones
Each has its own sequence of microtones
Together they make up a kind of tune
Your tune
The ceiling and walls are star maps
Breathing, alive
Those aren't stars, darling
That's your nervous system
Nanna didn't take you to planetariums like this
Go on, touch
Lovely, isn't it
Like phosphorus on Thule Lake
Sweet summer midnights
Shimmery, like applause under the skin
Can you make it out
Almost a hiss
An old shellac LP of white noise
Playing in the distance
Foolish, troublesome boy
That hapless adventuring of yours

Be very still
Now can you hear it

CHAPTER 12

(INGRAM MARSHALL, *FOG TROPES*)

[3 P.M.]

Loss leaders in shop windows,
fog spilling down the slopes
of Corona Heights, Twin Peaks, Tank Hill—

my name on everyone's lips:

—*August*, they say,
with resignation and dismay,
pulling up their collars against the wind.

On the wall of the darkened hallway,
not long before dawn,
horns baying out by the rocks,
trading calls as if lost, seeking one another out,
by the cliffs, sometimes in the key of G,
sometimes in the key of C,
depending on how the wind is blowing,
muffled by fog—
"All Blues" through a Harmon mute . . .

The same, and the same again . . .

The oboist upstairs—
why does he insist on practicing during my afternoon nap?

Why does it always have to be Ravel?

The *dead zone*—

headlights catch the fog pooling round the tires
of oncoming traffic.

All-Star break, midsummer,
football still eight weeks away:
you hear it in the voice of the radio sports talk host,

the pitch half an octave higher,
the rush of words, the combativeness,
no one calling in but the hard cases,

the same sad, old bachelors,
chewing the cud, chewing the cud, chewing . . .

[WIND/WORK]

The sound of the wind awakens me,
I cannot say what time,
but in the depths of night.
I can tell by the absence of street noise.

The gusts seem to arrive in sequences of three,
two short, one long—
violent anapests, the last the most protracted
and fierce,
gaining in force over its duration,
tossing the big palm's crown of fronds
until they crackle,
bending back the top of its trunk.
The building itself trembles.

Then a few minutes of calm until the next rush
of wind, each sequence more intense
than the last until it finally blows itself out.

From my Cabinet of Timbres
I remove two viols, one treble, one bass, a theorbo,
chitarrone, violin and, bless her,
here comes Ludmilla from the front room
wheeling the chamber organ down the hall.

I draw my bath,
as I do every morning this time of year
with the world outside having disappeared
but for the greenery out back, foregrounded,
bobbing and trembling in the stiff sea wind.

I shall have my chord,
even if I have to sit here soaking in this dark room

the entire morning.

        Schmelzer, Biber, Kapsberger—

it's in there somewhere

among the toccatas, sonatas, chaconnes.

I know because I have heard it there before.

CHAPTER 42

(CASPIAN LAKE, VERMONT)

Those French boys in the engine room aren't giving him much,
but he doesn't need much, does Carlos Wesley Byas of Muskogee, Oklahoma,
elbows on the bar at the Beaulieu, circa '47: —*I was born under the sign of
    music,*
he tells whoever's listening. That feathery tone of his by way of Hawk
but something else entirely, running through this set of ballads: "Laura,"
"Where or When," "Flamingo," unmistakable, no one played ballads like him.
Can't recall just where, Club Mephisto maybe, or the Vieux Colombier.
I've never seen the lake this still, Stannard Mtn. across the way dissolving
    into mist,
then gone completely as night settles in, just as he's finishing up with "Stardust."
You can begin to make out a hint of bite in the air now, a couple of weeks
before you close the place down for the summer and head back to Boston,
or was it Brooklyn by then? I can't remember just when except it was delicious,
sitting there in the dark beside you, saying nothing, no need for old friends
to say much of anything at all by this point, staring out into the darkness,
finishing our drinks before heading back to the house for dinner.
Forgive me all this sentiment, but you were never one to shy from sentiment,
refined in manner, as one finds T'ang and Sung poets: *In my younger days I
never / Tasted sorrow. I wanted / To become a famous poet. / I wanted to get ahead /
So I pretended to be sad. / Now I am old and have tasted every sorrow, /
And I am content to loaf / And enjoy the clear autumn.* [Hsin Ch'i-Chi] or Tu Fu's
"Restless Night" or "Full Moon," ever since you first read Pound's *Cathay* at
    nineteen.
You'd always return to that well for refreshment, as have so many of us.

But we sit there a while longer until the loons take up their nocturnal chorus
as if on cue, almost directly on the heels of night's arrival, and a while after
   that.
This disc always tears me up whenever I hear it these days,
not to be sharing it, sitting beside you at sunset, autumn coming on.

CHAPTER 3

(THE MAGIC FLUTE)

Flynn fell off the cable car
and landed on his head.
                    Poor Flynn,
hardly Flynn anymore,
in a dinghy listing to starboard.

Flynn on his stool,
holding court down the block
at the Magic Flute,
his hound at his feet while the old LPs
hissed and popped through the weekend:

Boccherini and Mississippi Fred,
the plucky chanteuse and gag tunes.

Flynn, with his mug of rum
and that faraway gaze—
a wryness at the eyes and mouth
frozen into a carapace
over some enormous hurt.

You see it in the look of old beatniks,
at their rituals
in the café and bar windows of North Beach,
solemnly playing cards at noon,

afflicted with some private wisdom
denied parturition.

Flynn, drunk and alone
in his shop weekday afternoons
with his binfuls of concerti
and wailing brass.
                    Alone with his dog
and his rum and the fog
coming in and too stiff
to get up and change the record.

And Flynn, with his secret poems
in a fancy red box,
thwarted and feverish and illustrated
by a suburban Beardsley,

whatever ache or shame
prettified, made diffuse, and tied
with a rhyme
like a ribbon around a present.
The ghost of him presiding
over those last lost afternoons
weeks after the earthquake,
laths and studs showing through
the walls, and plaster
sprinkling the ancient Vocalions.

Now a consortium's gone and bought the block
and the old place has a brand-new front

with black glass,
very minimal, very flash,
and sells computer software.

And Flynn drifts further and further to sea
in a bed for old strays at Laguna Honda.

CHAPTER 4

(THE MONKEY OF LIGHT)

I. CLAVECIN POUR LES YEUX

The reader may know of the Jesuit Father Lewis Bernard Castel, renowned for his *"clavecin pour les yeux"* and his discovery of *"l'art de peindre les sons,"* the art of painting sound. What could be so ingenious as to render sound visible and make the eyes confident of all the pleasures that music can bring to the ears? Music has always, throughout time, found comparison with color, but it was the German Kircher, a man with a *geometrical* mind, who first deduced that what was perceptible to the ears might also be made perceptible to the eyes. This phenomenon, as it relates to music, he called "the monkey of light."

Father Castel, much taken by the notion of the *simian lucis*, began in earnest his work on the "ocular harpsichord," and twenty years later, on the twenty-first of December, 1755, the day of Saint Thomas, patron saint of the Incredulous and Harpsichords, this learned Jesuit, who had handed out an invitation to fifty persons of rank, some from abroad, lighted not less than one hundred candles.

II. CLAVECIN POUR LE VOYAGE

Well, the result was much commented upon at the time, this remarkable instrument of Father Castel's. But there were those, outside the circles that matter, where the ladies carry bouquets so that the perfume might mingle happily with the powder on their hair, and one in particular, a certain Migrenne, who were not content with the father's "pretty divagations" and sought to bring braver purpose to his invention.

Of this Migrenne, I shall say not too much. He was known to be a Freemason, even a friend of Mozart. As to the rest, the details are hidden from us, except to say that this Migrenne heard colors; that is, a certain chord might appear to him a yellowish orange, and when played an octave higher, turn almost white, but with overtones of pale green and violet. It was Migrenne's ambition to sit down at the instrument and illuminate the entire map of the world, including all of its Perus, Japanias and Archipelagos.

Have you ever seen the machines people carry about in the streets that show *curiosities* or *rarities* through a glass? By pulling little strings, scenes of Cities, Castles, Wars and everything you wish for may be brought before your eyes. Migrenne by moving his fingers, like a god, along the keyboard, with its sharps made of ebony and its naturals of bone, would set out to play the world into being, coloring it as his imaginings prompted, almost dreaming it into being, note by note.

On the inside lid of any good French harpsichord it is usual to find a painting: Cupid and Psyche, Castor and Pollux, perhaps chinoiserie: Chinese smoking and fiddling in a garden, that sort of thing. Orpheus charming the beasts: this is an especially popular motif. Migrenne, with his timbres, dusty, moist or lute-like, tart as a green apple or chocolaty, would paint over the gods and goddesses, the putti, castles and bergerie, and bring forth in their place his Africas, his Capes and Plateaus. And by applying certain pedal tones on the instrument, making a sarabande move dolefully, or by appoggiatura, a certain chromaticism or an especially brisk toccata, our friend Migrenne would temper or modulate as he went.

Clouds he would color myrrh, sometimes crimson, or for variety an agate or *pigeon neck*. Smoke, sails and flags were always blue bice and castles red lead. Of trees, some he made grass green, others burnt umber. Rome was pale rose and ochre. Tiles he colored vermillion, spires and pinnacles blue. The seashore and lakes were indigo. Ships amber, Spain saffron, but in places a thin wash of brown. Most principal towns and cities were carmine, the hills surrounding them gamboge. Brazil was pink and blue and red, like parrots. Meadows straw color. The sea a pale celadon.

You know the story of Daphne and the laurel tree. These were living maps. Migrenne brought into creation, wet and breathing: the Burgundian ambience entire, the roofs of Antwerp a copper green. In sequence of note and phrasing he played islets and downs, gold-topped basilicas, the sea boiling away at the edge of the Moluccas.

Music is fugitive, living a moment and leaving nothing behind. So it was these maps of Migrenne would pass by quickly before one's eyes, only to disappear without a trace. As to their verisimilitude and utility, one surely would be able to find his way among the cities, shrines and entrepôts, and through the wilderness between. But these maps had little to do with exactness of latitude. Rather, the estimable Migrenne put a prism over this world, in order to color it with his playing, visiting any one place only so long as the reverberation of a single plucked string.

("COMING ON THE HUDSON": WEEHAWKEN)

He seldom spoke, even when well, and when he did it was *misterioso*, brief,
a gnomic shorthand, often only a grunt,
but his musicians got it, Nellie, Boo Boo, and Sphere III too.
Nowadays next to nothing comes out his mouth, nothing at all.
—*What's with his head, Woo?*
(He insisted on calling all his doctors "Ping Pock Woo," can't say why)
—*Dunno*, says Woo.
A Steinway, marooned, in a corner of the living room.
Him mostly in the bedroom. Nica's cats pad in and out,
licking themselves clean where they've collapsed in a puddle of sunshine.
Still, he carefully dresses every morning, spiffed up, suit and tie,
only to stay lying there in bed, glued to Bob Barker and *The Price Is Right*:
the dinette sets and double-door Amana refrigerators,
brought to you by 100% pure Dove soap and Imperial margarine.
Tugs push garbage scows south to the harbor's mouth and open sea.
He watches the river all the day long. That's what he does:
what the wind and light make of the water, for seasons on end,
the shimmer off the river at 9 a.m., the wakes the ferries and cruise ships
    make—
headed where? Barbados? The Antilles? France?—
slowly passing across his field of vision like giant oceangoing wedding cakes.
What is there left to say, anyhow? Or play? They either got it or not.
His world, or what of it that's stayed with him, lies directly across the way:
the tenements of the old San Juan Hill neighborhood, Minton's, 52nd Street—
none of it what it was, everything something else . . .

He watches as the lights begin to switch on across the river come end of day,
the skyline and clouds above going electric with pinks and reds
as the sun goes down behind him over the Meadowlands in the west.
Sometimes at night, looking across, he feels a twinge, the throb and pull of it.
But it don't pull all that hard, and it's too damn much of a bother anyhow.

CHAPTER 40

(E X I L E)

The Super Chief speeds across the American West.
Herr Doktor Professor Von Geist pulls the ends of his mustache,
almost like a seabird
maneuvering its wings in unsettled weather,
while he gazes out at the desolation and tumbleweed—
the *echo-less-ness*, as that bore Krenek likes to put it—
moon drifting in and out of the clouds.
With a formal solemnity, confused perhaps
with dignity, along with the deliberateness
of a surgeon, he runs his fork
through the orange emulsion covering his salad,
or what they call here salad.

>   *—Anything wrong, sir?*
asks the Black waiter,
who, the celebrated musicologist notes,
bears more than a passing resemblance to Louis Jordan,
that would be Louis Jordan of jump band fame,
not the other.

And upon arrival he'll no doubt suffer Ernst
dragging him to *Kaffe und Kuchen* at Alma's,
loathsome Alma (what sort of man
keeps company with an ex-mother-in-law?).
The old Wien crowd on hand: Toch, Korngold, Bruno Walter,
even *verruckt* Otto,

glowering down from a great height, while outside
in this *urban Tahiti,*
this *Mausoleum of Easy-Going,*

the blooms in violet and grape colors
that look as if made of crepe paper, the traffic,
the ceaseless radio ads, the ubiquitous aroma of car exhaust,
of Cashmere Bouquet and barbecued meat,
this *Catalonian Plain*
of squat bungalows with semi-detached garages,
under the glare of the *Egyptian sun*
kept at bay, somewhat, by the closed venetian blinds.

Then Alma, after a pint or so
of Benedictine, locking eyes with poor Twelve-Tone Leverkühn
(who accosted Frau Feuchtwanger at the Brentwood Country
        Mart:
—*No, I am* not *a syphilitic!*)
regales the squirming genius with a list
of her celebrated amours:
—*Kokoshcka, my darling Otto, dragged a life-size model of me*
on his travels, lest he miss me too unbearably much;
and Berg, his Wozzeck, *as well you know,*
is dedicated to me;
then there was Gropius, my devoted slave.
But the most interesting personality I have known
quite naturally, was Mahler,
gazing contemptuously at poor Werfel,
—*Mein fetter dicklippiger Jude.*
At which point Alma Mahler-Werfel, later to become

Alma Werfel-Mahler,

produces, with a flourish, a lock of Beethoven's hair.

The story of which we shall save for another day.

(ROSE EXILE)

The parade floats trundle north along South Orange
in the clammy darkness and floral decay of pre-dawn Pasadena,
turning right onto the long stretch of Colorado Boulevard,
following exactly the parade route of the celebrated Tournament of Roses.

Burbling from speakers hidden in the palms and sycamores
one can, just, make out the *aching majesty* of Richard Wagner's
Siegfried Idyll and *Rhine Journey*, Furtwängler—who else—
conducting the Wiener Philharmoniker.

First, in perfect scale, bright vinyl fringe bedecking the bottom,
a bungalow-size replica of the Vienna Court Opera
is followed by yet another float, the Café Griensteidl, also from "Old Wien,"
with its Jugendstil lamps and marble-topped tables.

A local bit player, having grown out his sideburns,
solemnly writes down notes on a stave, while nibbling a Sacher torte:
Richard Strauss, let us say, at work on an opera.
And what are we now to think of Richard Strauss?

Following next, on a platform atop a huge frankfurter float,
comes the co-author of the *Dialectic of Enlightenment*,
seated behind a desk and clapping his hands to his ears
in a mechanical fashion, not unlike a wind-up toy.

This is not the desk later memorialized on Adorno-Platz in Bockenheim
but the desk from his Brentwood home at 316 South Kenter
(just a few doors down from the O.J. unpleasantness years later),
the tall, elaborate Bismarck-era monstrosity

with its multitude of small drawers and, beside it, the carved wooden chair
on which the great man now sits, in extreme agitation, crying out:
Wo die Aura ist? Wo die Aura ist?
The source of his distress is standing directly to his right

in a form-fitting sequined gown, singing in a voice one critic described as
trumpet-clean, pennywhistle piercing, Wurlitzer wonderful.
You will know of whom I'm speaking.
It is the "brass diva" herself, Miss Ethel Merman,

belting out a hair-raising version of "I Get a Kick Out of You."
"What's with the long face, Pudge?" she growls,
realizing she has not moved Wiesengrund-Adorno, not one eeny-weeny bit.
"Loosen up and live a little, Mr. Big Shot Wisenheimer."

At this moment bombers are assembling into their formations over Europe.
Dishes on their rubber racks are almost now completely dry.
Someone is inventing color TV.
Millions of cans of corn niblets sit in the darkness on shelves across the Midwest.

The streets remain empty.
The circumstances had been made clear to the participants at the start.
Trucks rumble in the distance across the Arroyo Seco,
while the first birds of the day, unbothered as ever, commence their singing.
(

CHAPTER 21

(A P R I L   I N   P A R I S)

(for Betsy Jolas)

. . . *chestnuts in blossom*, you know,
the Sarah Vaughan version, where Clifford Brown
comes in halfway through
like the Sun King into a rumpled, smoky bedroom . . .

In the hotel elevator
with its worn plush and elaborate fittings
a Tadd Dameron large band arrangement
circa 1950-something
comes out of the overhead speaker
as if poured through history's electrified sieve.

The art of the *American Negro Jazz Musician*
is much beloved here
among this enlightened and tolerant race
with their stylized, birdlike gestures
and agile little faces.
            —*Hello there*,
says the Black man with the trumpet
to the chestnut vendor, circa 1950-something,
receiving a wave and hearty greeting.

Outside, along the boulevards,
stanchions and chestnuts surpliced with posters;
it is election time:

              M. Bon Temps Roule vs. The Major,
both villains,
both, too, acquainted with a certain Nathalie,
dark and playful Nathalie,
four flights up, second door on the left.
She has a favorite compilation, this one,
some lightly throbbing *Chaabi*
along with a brooding jazz film score
circa . . .

Operas, revolutions, outrages at the Salon—
c'est complet.
          A small new museum
is soon to open near the Quai American Negro Jazz Musician,
with photos of the many visiting greats—
Dameron, Brown, et al.—
posing with their arms around the chestnut vendor
and the darkly pretty girl, a favorite
among the musicians, a certain Nathalie.

They are all waving heroically
that chilly, gray afternoon by the river,
like something out of Géricault.
No, make that Doisneau.
They are waving at the photographer,
probably, also, to a small crowd of fans,

and, unwittingly, even to us,
who stare back at them impassively
from behind our screens.

CHAPTER 81

(S A R A N A C   L A K E)

Beautiful Béla,
birdlike, frail and wan, and those unforgettably luminous blue eyes
so often remarked upon, by his students especially, young Solti, Földes, others,
the first thing most noticed about him,
now wrapped against the chill in his dark cloak,
in the garden outside his tiny cabin in Saranac Lake, spartan as a peasant
    cottage.
He is notating birdsong and calculating the vibrations of a hummingbird:
—*My result is about ninety to one hundred per second.*

—*Spring has now indisputably arrived*, he writes to his son Peter:
A kind of dogwood in bloom that resembles the acacias at home,
the birds completely drunk with it, putting on concerts
the like of which I've never heard.

puty . puty . puty ./ ./ ./.

Always of delicate constitution, even in the vigor of his younger days,
traveling through the Carpathian Basin with his great friend Kodály,
the only real relationship he ever had,
gathering folk songs, recording the shepherds on their pan pipes.
Schizothymic, Zoltán described him:

fragile, fine, sensitive, withdrawn,

unyielding, awkward, lonely, ascetic . . .

Close to death now, incorporeal, inhabited only by the pure spirit of music,
he struggles to complete Piano Concerto no. 3, for Ditta, his farewell,
all but seven bars left unorchestrated; Tibor will finish the job.
Listen to the second movement, the *Adagio religioso*,
when the birds come in, four minutes and thirty seconds in:
the eastern towhee, the hermit and wood thrush—
oboe, flute, piano, clarinet and piccolo.
Apart from his Bach, Schumann, Liszt, Debussy and the rest
he seemed only able to tolerate the sounds of animals, birds, insects.
In the city he was tormented by the car horns, jackhammers, radios,
physically distressed by the noise. He had been like that since a small child.
The "chickmucks," as he called them, especially delighted him,
their soft trills, the chipping, and a pitch lower, their clucking sound.

. . . *severe, withdrawn, systematic, precipitate, aristocratic, mistrustful.*

—*I never much cared for his music*, Stravinsky would later volunteer.

CHAPTER 6

(ODEON)

The young Villa-Lobos, of *bold and robust temperament*,
silently runs his bow across the strings of his cello
until, when he can no longer resist, he joins in
as Ernesto Nazareth continues his piano improvisations
in the lobby of the Odeon movie house,
featuring musical animation cinema *cum* refreshments,
tango after tango, none alike, always fresh, issuing
from what seems a boundless store of invention,
by the dozens, almost never written down,
each a glistening jewel, a refined sort of bordello piano
aspiring, perhaps, to higher art, that Heitor, twenty years later,
will carry with him to the musical salons of Paris,
cannibal music, these tangos and choros of his
with their hidden savors of Africa,
tone colors of the Amazon rainforest:
yellow-ridged toucans, tree frogs, howler monkeys,
suggested but not quite heard.

It is terribly hot, the ceiling fans nearly useless,
elegant clientele sweating
like overtaxed beasts of burden,
the men in their white shirts, ties and coats,
the women in long cotton dresses, daintily fanning themselves.
Belle Époque Rio, with its handsome three-story buildings
and wrought iron balconies, French Rio,

grand promenades with their profusion of shade trees,
where the fashionable make their way from the Praça XV docks
to the city center, the women dressed in a parody
of *haute couture*, outlandish coquettes, pausing
at the ice-cream and confectionary shops,
at the windows of elegant clothing stores along Ouvidor Street:
horse-drawn trams, the new wonder of electricity,
faint sounds of a pianoforte in the background,
beautiful Black women with gold jewelry and precious stones,
yellow fever, samba percolating in the hills.

At one table sits Claudel from the French embassy
with his friend Milhaud, butterball genius, recently arrived
from Marseilles, whom he had invited down
expressly to *listen*. And he does, intently and with fascination,
intrigued most by the rhythms and polyrhythms,
the delayed downbeats, the weave of ostinatos:
an imperceptible suspense,
a languorous breath, a subtle pause,
almost impossible to recapture. The "little nothing," he calls it,
on this sultry afternoon
in the lobby of a movie theater on Avenida Rio Bravo:

        fluido, apaixonado, triste

(ROUTE 4)

Coltrane just sits there,
almost expressionless, thoughtful, perhaps even a touch somber,
on the little red stool in my bedroom, listening to the Dodger radio broadcast
from Ebbets Field. We speak not at all.
Occasionally, he might lift an eyebrow when Vin Scully raises his voice
if Duke blasts one out or Gino Cimoli guns down a runner going for second.
He is a handsome man with a well-shaped head, but a bit puffy around the eyes
like in the cover photo of *A Love Supreme*, but this is earlier, '57 or so.

It's evening, after dinner, the family downstairs, doing what they do.
John will come by now and then to sit with me
on his way back from Van Gelder's studio in Hackensack
after recording all day. Art Taylor or Red Garland might drop him off here
on their way back into the city. Usually, they all just hop on a bus,
the #162 to the uptown bus terminal near Columbia Presbyterian.
Are you familiar with his composition "Route 4," the highway they travel?
It really *moves*.

I never know when John will turn up, but I'm always happy when he does,
more than happy. Mom and Dad seem amenable to his visits,
even Grand, very out of character, who barks like mad when the doorbell rings.
In some ways John Coltrane has replaced Grand,
who would sit watchfully beside me when I was smaller still, my guardian.
When John's on hand it's like Grand's night off, and he flops down
under the living room coffee table for an extended nap

near my folks, who are reading *The Atlantic Monthly* or John O'Hara, like that.

Can't remember them ever listening to jazz or even knowing who Coltrane is,

just this exceedingly polite and kind young Black man

who enjoys sitting with Aug and keeping him company, nothing odd about that.

I really can't recall when exactly these visits first began

but they remain vivid in my memories of childhood,

like snow days playing with my toy soldiers or the aroma of Hiram's hot dogs

    frying in deep fat,

and remain most comforting. Even today, all these years later,

whenever I'm a bit off or in need of something, I don't quite know what,

I play his Prestige sides from 1957, "Russian Lullaby" or "Traneing In,"

and think of my friend, John Coltrane, just sitting there beside me, listening.

CHAPTER 31

(BAY LULLABY)

Tuesdays are bad for sausage and flowers
rain
sweeping in off the sea, foghorns
lowing like outsize beasts
shackled to cliffs at the mouth of the Bay

You hear them from under the movie marquee
before going in to dry
off in plush, alone
behind two old ladies, that song of a wanton from long ago
"Temptation," filling the empty room

Across the city's northwest quadrant
two, maybe three miles in
drifting through holes in the traffic and rain
you hear them warning ships off the rocks
moaning like fettered gods

Lilies begun to curl
and meat gone sad at the delicatessen
trays of wurst
fat seeping into the skins
before Thursday delivery and the big weekend

As morning's first trolley clears the track
the cat's petit snores
my love's upper lip beaded with sweat
you can still hear them out there in the dark
mingling their calls in the rain

(FINIS)

Like the faint sound of thunder, rumbling in the distance, then gathering in
volume

until, with a great roar, it all comes crashing down, an avalanche of Europe's
concert halls,

like the 7.4 cubic kilometer chunk of the Jacobshavn glacier, calving into the
sea below:

the red and Alaska yellow cedar stages and smoked birch parquet floors, a
reverberating crack,

splintering on the rocks below, seals clapping, barking *CHUM CHUM,
CHUM CHUM*:

the balconies and loggias, walls paneled in vertical grain, plaster and gypsum
board,

cherrywood acoustic panels, the Cologne Gürzenich, the Festspielhaus and
Mozarteum,

the Teatro della Pergola, the Graf-Zeppelin-Haus, the Grosser
Musikvereinssaal,

crashing and splintering on the rocks below, then sliding into the sea;

the gilt of the Palais Garnier with its Chagall ceiling, the staircases of the
Staatsoper,

the neoclassical facades and baroque rotundas, the Mariinsky, Barcelona's
Gran Teatre del Liceu

splintering on the rocks below and crashing into the sea. *CHUM CHUM,
CHUM CHUM*, they bark.

A further rumbling and here they come, a second avalanche of chamber
    ensembles and string quartets:
There's Suk, Dvořák's son-in-law,
                arms and legs akimbo, bow in his right hand, Strad in his left,
        like the "falling man" of the Twin Towers,
                            in what seems like slow motion,
        falling into the maw of nothingness: the dichroistic flames of the violin
            turning from gold to dark red as he falls
                            into echoless space. And on his heels:
                    Oistrakh, then Marsick and Carl Flesch,
                    the old Euro-Men in their monkey suits
and high, starched collars,
            the fistula of a rotten, paternalistic culture, *an old bitch gone in the teeth*,
                    burst and spewing pus:
            plates   ribs   necks   and   scrolls,
                    a rain of spruce bellies, maple backs
            black-dyed pear purls, white poplar sandwiched between,
    the fittings, pegs, tailpieces,
                    ebony, rosewood, Oregon mahogany,
            seasoned for ten years.
HERE COMES EVERYBODY:
        the Lerner, Pro Arte, Budapest and Busch,
                    the Ysaÿe, the Kolisch, Prague and Bohemian:
Auer, Yankelevich, Yampolsky,
                snow on the Neva, the clank of steam pipes in the recital hall
                (spare me, please, this sentimental tosh),
        stifling, bombastic, hothouse scum,
                        temperamental, over-rehearsed neurotics,
        lackeys, degenerates, playthings of the *haut bourgeois* . . .

Mao would have known what to do with them . . .

CHUM CHUM, CHUM CHUM, they bark,

        beside themselves, raucous with bloody-eyed glee . . .

ACKNOWLEDGMENTS

The author wishes to thank the editors of the *London Review of Books*, where all but a handful of these poems first appeared.